PRIDE OF INDIA

VOLUME 1

ADAPTED FROM ORIGINAL
AMAR CHITRA KATHA COMICS

PRIDE OF INDIA

VOLUME 1

ADAPTED FROM ORIGINAL
AMAR CHITRA KATHA COMICS

WRITTEN BY
Pika Nani

TIMELESS
Amar Chitra Katha

RUPA

Published by
Rupa Publication India Pvt. Ltd.
7/ 16, Ansari Road, Daryaganj, New Delhi 110002

First published by Rupa Publication India Pvt. Ltd.
In collaboration with Amar Chitra Katha Pvt. Ltd. 2024

Sales centres:
Bengaluru, Chennai
Hyderabad, Jaipur, Kathmandu
Kolkata, Mumbai, Prayagraj

AMAR CHITRA KATHA PVT LTD
Office no. 5017/18/19/20
1AEROCITY NIBR Corporate Park
Andheri East, Sakinaka
Mumbai 400072

Art Director – Ketan Tondwalkar
Designed by Manoj Tandel

Adapted from the original ACK Comics
Original Illustrations
Mother Teresa – Atul Siriwardane
Mahatma Gandhi – Souren Roy
A P J Abdul Kamal – Arijit Dutta Chowdhury

P-ISBN: 978-93-6156-357-7
E-ISBN: 978-93-6156-617-2

First impression 2024

10 9 8 7 6 5 4 3 2 1

Printed in India

CONTENTS

A.P.J. Abdul Kalam

"I want to fly someday!" Abdul said with a quiet determination in his voice. The fifteen-year-old was standing on the edge of a rocky shore. The wind blew his dark wavy hair and a blue sea stretched endlessly in front of him. But the young boy's eyes were fixed on a flock of squawking seagulls flying overhead. He was on a field trip from school, and his teacher was explaining the technique used by birds to fly. Something stirred in Abdul; his

eyes shone – a dream to fly was born! The boy with the dream was none other than our beloved and respected 11th president of India, A.P.J. Abdul Kalam!

He was born on 15th October, 1931, in Rameswaram, a tiny island off the southern tip of Tamil Nadu. The Pamban Bridge was the only road connecting it to the mainland. Yet, it was a bustling pilgrimage centre, as according to the Ramayana, it was here that Lord Rama had built a bridge to go to Lanka and rescue his wife, Sita. People flocked to the famous Ramanathaswamy temple, which was near Abdul's house.

Abdul's father, Jainulabdeen, was the Imam of the local mosque. As a child Abdul learnt about the importance of faith and prayer from him. The chanting of hymns from the temple and the call for prayer from the mosque created a singular harmony in young Abdul's mind. He grew up believing that the 'One' listening was the same God. In his mind all faiths became one.

Once, his father took up a project to build a boat to ferry pilgrims from Rameswaram to a nearby town. Abdul, who was six years old then, would often help him out in the project. It was here that he struck an unusual friendship with Jalal and Shamsuddin, who were many years his senior.

He was an inquisitive child and asked many questions: "How do birds fly?" and "Why does water fall from the sky?"

Jalal laughed. "Someday you will learn, Abdul. There is so much out there."

"Out where?"

"In the world outside, away from this little island," sighed Jalal. "Someday you will spread your wings and fly!"

While the older boys spent the evenings reading the newspaper and discussing

current events, Abdul listened to them and looked at the pictures.

Jalal was the only person on the island who could read and write a little bit of English. He would often get requests from people to write their job applications and official letters.

Observing Jalal, Abdul would think, "I want to be like him one day." This was perhaps the first stirring of desire in his heart for knowledge and respect.

By the time Abdul was eight years old, the ripple effects of the Second World War were being felt in his remote village as well. Food was being rationed and money was tight. Even though he was the youngest among five children, Abdul wanted to help his mother, Ashiamma, by earning a few annas. There was a demand for tamarind seeds, so Abdul began collecting and selling them in his free time.

One day, as he was chatting with Jalal, Shamsuddin turned up looking gloomy.

"You look worried. What is the matter?" asked a concerned Abdul.

"The train delivering the newspapers is not going to stop at Rameswaram anymore!" he cried. "My business is over." Shamsuddin was the only newspaper agent in town.

"That means we won't get newspapers from now on!" Abdul exclaimed.

Jalal had an idea. "Calm down! Can't someone throw the papers out to you from the train?"

"Yes, but I will need someone fast enough to catch them," said Shamsuddin, stroking his chin.

"Don't worry, I will do it," Abdul said with lot of confidence.

The next day Abdul rushed to the station, out of breath. He had woken up at four that morning to attend math tuitions. Then his father had taken him to the Arabic school, where he learnt the Quran Sharif. As he reached the platform, a shrill whistle sounded. Puffs of smoke rose from the engine. The train rattled through without pause.

"I'm here! Throw the bundle," Abdul shouted and waved at the man on the train with the stack of newspapers.

Whoosh! The bundle came flying and the young boy caught it neatly. He then ran around town delivering the papers. It was eight by the time he reached home for breakfast and headed to school. While most of his classmates were starting their day, Abdul was halfway through his!

After school, he went around town again collecting the newspaper dues and gave them to Shamsuddin, who paid him his daily wages.

The moment Abdul reached home he handed the money to his mother. "Here, Amma, today's earnings."

"Abdul, my big little boy." Ashiamma smiled, giving him a hug.

It was a tough year for Abdul. His schedule was exhausting, but the pride and joy in his mother's eyes kept him going.

Abdul studied at Schwartz High School, went to college in Tiruchirappalli, and then studied at the Madras Institute of Technology. He was worried his father wouldn't be able to afford the fees for M.I.T. His eldest and only sister, Zohra, came to the rescue. "Here, take my gold bangles. Sell them for your fees, dear Abdul."

"No, Zohra! What are you saying?" Abdul protested. He knew that the bangles were the only jewellery his sister possessed.

Jalal who had married Zohra and was now his brother-in-law, also persuaded him. "She is right! You must study further. That is our only wish."

Deeply touched, he pawned the bangles and worked hard to get a scholarship and redeem them.

At M.I.T Abdul studied aeronautical engineering and began to pursue his dream of flying in earnest. He worked hard to become more self-confident and a better communicator. By his final year he had established himself as a promising student.

Abdul was assigned a project to design an attack aircraft. But when the professor saw his design, he was angry and tore up the paper. "I am very disappointed that a talented person like you has come up with this," he scolded. "I want a new design by Monday or you will lose your scholarship."

"But it is already Friday evening, sir! This work took a month," pleaded a visibly shaken Abdul.

The professor gave a final ultimatum, "Two days or you go home."

Abdul put aside his doubts and set to work. He knew he could not go home now, after having come so far.

He worked non-stop and recreated a month's work by Sunday evening.

The professor was impressed. "I set you an impossible deadline and you have come up

with your best work." He patted Abdul on the back. "I knew I was pushing you, but I had to make you recognise your true potential."

Abdul realised that a teacher who knew how to make you excel was a true friend and that there was no such thing as an impossible deadline. Both lessons would help him through life.

After graduation in 1960, Abdul went to Dehradun to try and join the Air Force. "I can't wait to fly! To make a machine rise higher and higher... Ah!" thought Abdul as he waited with the other candidates for the results. But he missed the seat by a whisker! He came in ninth, while there were only eight seats. His dreams of flying had come crashing down.

But as it often happens in life, when one door closes, another one opens. Abdul went back to Delhi and found out that he had been accepted at the Directorate of Technical

Development and Production (DTD&P) Air, as a senior scientific assistant. He consoled himself that though he couldn't fly planes he could at least help to make them.

***

The 60s were a heady time for rocketry in the country. The dream was to put India on the space map. It was at this important juncture that Abdul joined INCOSPAR (later known as ISRO, or the Indian Space Research Organisation) as a rocket engineer. He was greatly inspired by the founder, Dr. Vikram Sarabhai, who was an iconic figure in science and a pioneer of India's space programme.

Abdul's first project was at the equatorial rocket launching station (TERLS) in Thumba, a fishing village in Kerala. What made the place special was that it was located close to the earth's magnetic equator.

Abdul arrived with his bags and stood on the beach, looking at an ancient church. It was a beautiful brick structure with towering spires, arched windows and a rusty bell.

"Are you sure we are in the right place?" asked Abdul in wonder as they stepped into

the assembly hall with a high-rafted roof and the statue of Mary Magdalene at the altar.

His colleague Sudhakar smiled and nodded. "Dr. Sarabhai and the Bishop convinced the people to give the place up for science.

They agreed that science and spirituality both work towards the same end – the prosperity of humans."

Abdul was impressed. "That is so true! I have also been greatly influenced by both. I have always felt they can co-exist."

Over the next few months Abdul got busy developing rockets, satellites and their launch vehicles under the leadership of Dr. Sarabhai. With his guidance Abdul grew as a scientist and a leader.

Abdul even got a chance to visit NASA – the National Aeronautics and Space Administration – on his first trip abroad.

Back at Thumba, one day Abdul and Sudhakar went to check on a dangerous chemical mixture. As Sudhakar bent over the container to inspect the mix, a single drop of sweat from his forehead fell into the highly inflammable chemical – and BOOM! The blast threw the men off their feet.

Everything was on fire! The rising flames were closing in on them, the smoke was making it difficult to breathe. Using great presence of mind, Sudhakar broke a window and pushed Abdul out before jumping out himself.

Later Abdul went to meet his injured friend at the hospital. "You saved my life before

thinking of your own. How can I repay you, dear Sudhakar?"

"Just make sure our work doesn't suffer," Sudhakar said with a smile.

Abdul was deeply moved. "Sudhakar, I am going to make sure my life was worth saving," he vowed.

By 1969 plans were underway to build an Indian Satellite Launching Vehicle (SLV). Sriharikota, a barrier island in Andhra Pradesh, was the chosen site. Abdul was the project leader and was later promoted to project director. He was designing, communicating, co-ordinating, analysing and solving problems. When asked how he managed to do everything, the budding poet in him answered, "If you want to leave your footprints on the sands of time, you cannot drag your feet."

The work was in full flow when tragedy struck. News came that Jalal had passed away. Abdul was disheartened. He did not feel like continuing with his work. In the next two years he lost his father and then his mother. As he sat in the mosque of his childhood, mourning their loss, he felt as if a divine voice spoke to him. "They carried out the task I designed for them with dedication and honesty and then came back to me. Why are you mourning their

day of accomplishment? Concentrate on your work and proclaim my glory through your deeds."

The next day Abdul returned to Thumba and immersed himself in work.

Soon the SLV-3 was ready for its first trial. Abdul's boss, Dr. Brahm Prakash, and the chairman of ISRO, Prof. Satish Dhawan, were present to witness the launch. The ground rumbled as the rocket took off, leaving behind a thick trail of vapour. Stage 1 was perfect! But stage 2 spiralled out of control. Instead of going higher, the SLV plummeted down and down, and fell into the sea with a big splash. There was shock and disbelief all around.

At the press conference, Prof. Dhawan took the blame for the failure. He said, "Yes, we have failed today. But I have full faith in my team. Within a year we will succeed."

True to their word, a year later, on 18th July, 1980, the SLV-3 was launched, carrying the Rohini satellite.

From the mission control room, Abdul announced with pride, "The Rohini satellite is in orbit!"

The man who never got to fly an aircraft had put a satellite into space. The entire nation erupted in joy.

During the press conference Prof. Dhawan asked Abdul to speak, giving him full credit for the success. Abdul was inspired by Prof. Dhawan's actions. He had taken responsibility for the failure, but he had attributed the success to the team. This shaped Abdul's idea of a true leader.

The launch of SLV-3 led India to enter an exclusive club of space-faring nations and played a great role in building India's space programme.

Abdul left ISRO in 1982 to join the missile laboratory of DRDO (Defence Research and Development Organisation). He worked along with the defence scientific advisor to the defence minister, Dr. V. S. R. Arunachalam, and other distinguished scientists, to draft an ambitious programme to make five indigenous missiles in India. This would take the country to the next level of defence preparedness.

A modern laboratory was built in Hyderabad, the Research Centre Imarat (RCI), which soon became a renowned centre of excellence.

Abdul was determined to recruit young blood for the project. "We need more and more young people to take over from us oldies," he would joke. Thus, began a drive where he and his team visited colleges all over the country, inviting fresh engineers and scientists to join them. Eventually, 280 youngsters became part of the project.

Trishul was the first missile to be launched in 1985. Then came Prithvi in 1988. It was a surface-to-surface missile that could strike a target with an accuracy of 50 metres.

It made the world sit up and take notice. The western world reacted with anger.

Dr. Arunachalam had bad news to deliver. "Abdul, seven countries have imposed a technology ban on us. Now we can't buy anything remotely connected with missiles."

"They cannot stomach the fact that India could

be self-reliant in this field. But we will show them we can produce missiles despite the ban," replied a confident Kalam.

More than 500 scientists and organisations across the country worked on Agni, the most ambitious missile project and Kalam's favourite.

The day of the launch, 20th April, 1989, arrived bright and clear. The countdown had begun. 18... 17... 16... 15... 14... when suddenly the computer screens began flashing 'HOLD'.

"Oh no, something is wrong!" cried Abdul. "Abort the launch!"

The scientists were disheartened, but Abdul motivated them to try again. "I saw my SLV vanish into the sea. You still have your missile in front of you. So, cheer up!"

Ten days later, Agni was to be launched again, but just before take-off, the same problem occurred and the launch had to be aborted.

The news of the failure spread quickly. The media made jokes, and Abdul and his team became the laughing stock of the nation.

Unfazed by the turn of events, Abdul called a meeting of his team. "We have been given a great opportunity," he began. "But great opportunities come with great challenges. The country deserves success from us. Let us aim to successfully launch Agni by the end of the month."

On 22nd May, 1989, Agni had a dream launch.

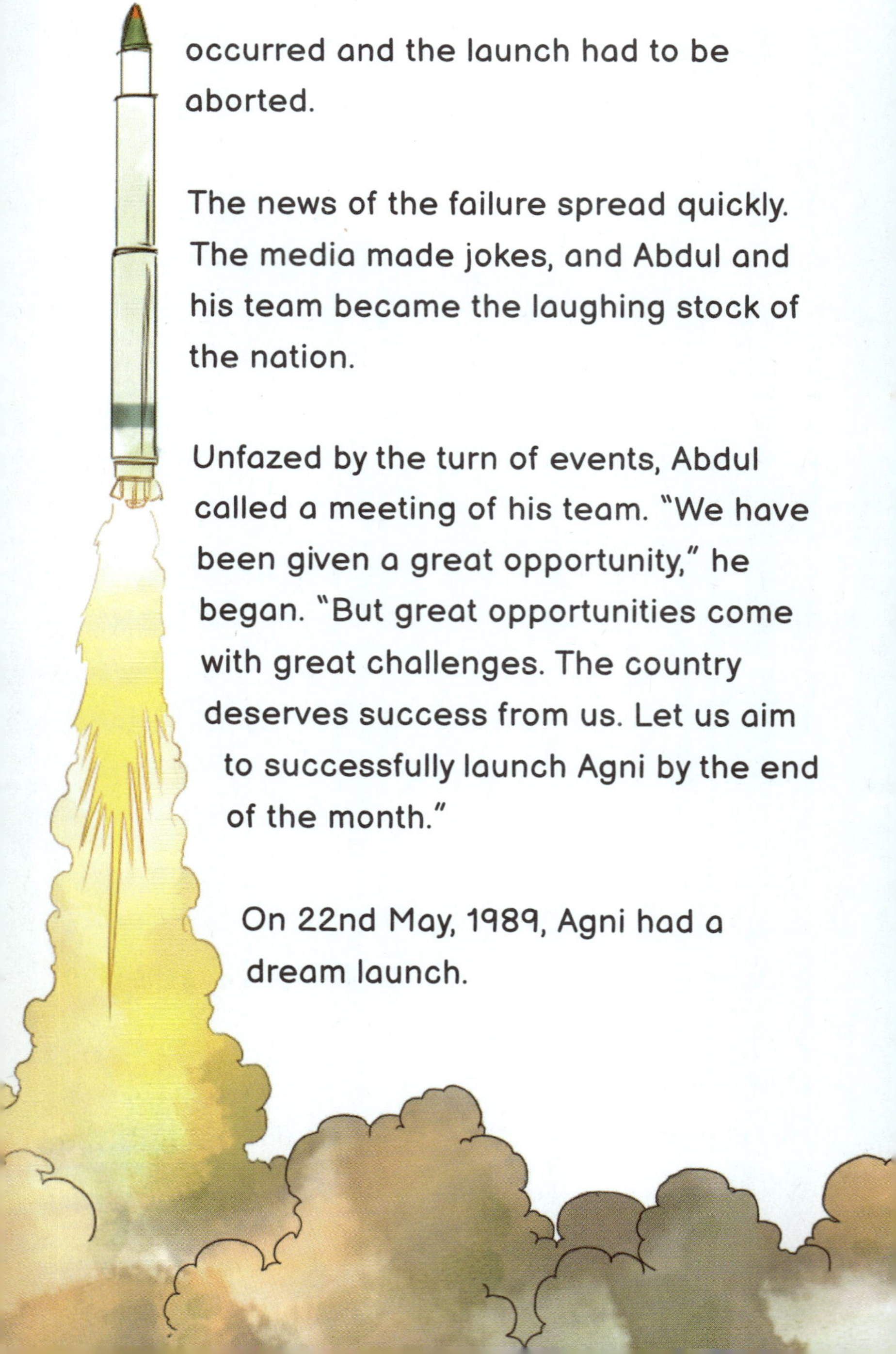

The entire country cheered as one and Agni became more than a missile – it became a symbol of pride for every Indian. People began calling Abdul Kalam the 'Missile Man of India'.

The following Republic Day, Kalam and Dr. Arunachalam were bestowed with the Padma Vibhushan for their achievements.

Abdul was using technology to empower defence forces. But he believed that technology should also be used to help people.

Working with a cardiologist, he used missile-grade steel to make stents for the heart. This brought the price down from Rs.75,000 to Rs.10,000.

The plight of polio-infected children struggling to walk with heavy metal braces made Abdul feel miserable. The scientist in him had to find a solution. Within weeks, Abdul and his team had produced braces that reduced the weight of the metal callipers from four kilos to a mere four hundred grams. Abdul had used the same materials that go into the making of lightweight missiles to make lightweight braces. Watching the children's faces as they moved around happily brought him great joy.

In 1992 Kalam succeeded Dr. Arunachalam as scientific advisor to the defence minister. He was awarded honorary doctorates from various universities and came to be called Dr. Abdul Kalam. The biggest honour came when he was awarded the Bharat Ratna, India's highest civilian award, in 1997.

All the recognition and honour could not change Abdul. He had learnt to make his voice heard, but at heart he was still a simple island boy.

***

The year was 1998. A small group of men wearing olive green shirts, trousers and hats were making their way slowly through the stunning and daunting sand dunes of the Thar desert in Rajasthan.

The air was dry, and the sun was beating down their backs, there was only sand as far as the eyes could see.

"Major General Prithviraj," called out a man.

The General did not stop.

"Prithviraj sir..." called the man again.

"Oh, you are calling me!" Abdul stopped and turned around. "The name Prithviraj suits me, doesn't it?" he smiled.

"But, sir, did we really need to wear army uniforms and have secret identities?" asked another scientist from his team.

"We are in an army range in Pokhran, about to carry out top-secret nuclear tests. So, yes, every precaution is necessary," replied Kalam. "And walking on these sand dunes has given me an idea."

That night, Abdul and his team got to work under a starry sky. They had chosen to work under the cover of night not to avoid the desert heat but to avoid the prying satellites of other countries.

"Pile mounds of earth to make them look like sand dunes," Abdul instructed the men digging the ground, preparing for the underground tests. "Any foreign satellite viewing us will not register our activity."

In the morning the team shifted back the equipment and concealed them. In this way Operation Shakti continued for many days.

Finally, on 11th May, 1998, the earth rumbled BOOM! BOOM! BOOM! Not one but three nuclear devices were detonated. The country woke up to the news of the test's great success. India was established as a nuclear power! Abdul Kalam was hailed as a hero!

Abdul knew the nuclear tests were important for the nation, but they weighed heavily on his mind. Taking inspiration from a spiritual guru, he started a new journey, to inspire and educate the children and youth of India. He believed that if they were taught well, tomorrow's world would be a peaceful one. He visited schools, colleges and institutions across the country, spreading his message. Children loved listening to his inspiring talks.

Abdul wanted to share whatever he had learnt in his journey of life with as many people as possible. This prompted him to write his autobiography, Wings of Fire, which was followed by a series of books, including Ignited Minds and Turning Point. All of them were instant bestsellers.

Once, on the way to meet children in Bokaro, the helicopter he was travelling in met with a minor accident. No one on board was hurt, but this second brush with death made Abdul realise that he wanted to devote his time to educating children and unfolding his vision for India.

Abdul left his job and was content to spend his days teaching. But destiny had other plans for him. In June 2002, he got a call from Prime Minister Atal Bihari Vajpayee. "Kalam, we would like to nominate you for the post of the president of India."

Abdul was lost for words. "Huh? But... but..."

"Think about it. I have to make the announcement tonight. You have two hours, but please say yes."

Abdul's mind was in a whirl. "Me... president? I am the simple son of a simple man, what do I know about politics?" he thought.

He spent the next two hours calling his friends and relatives. Opinion was divided.

"You are already doing what you love. Why disturb it?" said some.

"This is a great opportunity! You can take your vision for India to the next level," said others.

Finally, Abdul decided to put his vision above himself and agreed.

On 25th July, 2002, he was sworn in as the eleventh president of our country in a grand ceremony held at the Central Hall of

Parliament. The guest list was as unusual as Abdul himself. Besides his family and colleagues, he had invited his old professors, the Imam of his Rameswaram mosque, the head of the Ramanathaswamy temple and the priest of the Rameswaram church. There were also a hundred children from different states of India.

Dr. Kalam moved from his humble abode to the most prestigious address in the country – the Rashtrapati Bhavan – with 340 rooms and 190 acres of gardens.

From day one it was clear that Kalam was going to bring about a sea change in the way things worked.

For his first meeting at Rashtrapati Bhavan, a long table had been set up with a throne-like chair at the head. "Good morning, your excellency," greeted a staff member, guiding him to the throne.

"Just Kalam, or you can call me Dr. Kalam if you wish," Abdul quipped and in his inimitable way he sat down on an ordinary chair.

Looking at the surprised faces all around, Abdul explained, "I know this is like a palace, but I want it to become a people's palace. People should feel their voices are being heard here and action is being taken. We are all the same; they should know that."

His position came with many privileges, but he remained true to his principles. Once when fifty of his family members came to visit him, he insisted on paying for their rent and food from his own savings.

Not only did he change the nature of the position, he also changed how work was done. Being a scientist and an academician, he realised that if everything was computerised, digitised and networked, work could get done faster. This led him to initiate e-governance in the Rashtrapati Bhavan.

During his tenure, Kalam was able to present his vision 2020 to the Parliament a number of times.

An important aspect of Abdul's vision was implementing P.U.R.A. – providing urban amenities in rural areas. P.U.R.A. village clusters had institutions, hospitals and employment opportunities spread across a group of villages well-connected by road. Abdul was so committed to this idea that he donated his life savings to the project.

By now Kalam had a special place in every Indian's heart and became the people's president. Everywhere he went, he was greeted by hordes of people, who sometimes waited all day to get a glimpse of him. He was a youth icon and his popularity led the media to give him the title of 'Rockstar'!

His fame had spread all around the world and his legendary speeches were met with thunderous applause.

On one such occasion, while addressing the parliament of the European Union, he said, "Where there is righteousness in the heart, there is beauty in the character. When there is beauty in the character, there is harmony in the home, when there is harmony in the home, there is order in the nation. When there is order in the nation, there is peace in the world." The writer and poet in him knew how to convey his ideas in the most impactful manner.

Being president meant that Dr. Kalam was also the supreme commander of the armed forces. He made it a point to visit his men posted in difficult terrains, from the Siachen glaciers to the Naval submarine, INS Sindhurakshak.

In June 2006 he visited an air force base in Pune. Abdul was taken to see the Sukhoi aircraft. The mission computers and all other equipments used in the aircraft had been made in India.

Abdul was admiring the Sukhoi when a memory stirred in him. "You know, I once dreamed of becoming a pilot. It was my biggest dream," he told the pilot wistfully.

"I could train you, sir. You could fly with me as co-pilot."

Never one to refuse a challenge, Abdul undertook the training.

On the day of the flight, he arrived at the tarmac looking smart in a blue G-suit, the anti-gravitational suit worn by fighter pilots in India. He waved to the crowd of onlookers and climbed into the cockpit.

His eyes were shining with excitement as they took off – higher and higher, the Sukhoi

soared. Soon he was flying at nearly twice the speed of sound.

"This was the most exciting half hour of my life!" Kalam said joyously on his return.

Not only did Abdul live his childhood dream that day, he also set a record – at 74, he was the oldest Indian to fly a fighter aircraft!

Truly there can be none other like A.P.J. Abdul Kalam – a scientist, a teacher, a writer, a poet, a president, a visionary – but most of all a humble and great human being.

Mother Teresa

South-eastern Europe was in great turmoil by 1910. The Ottoman Empire, which had controlled the region for centuries, was on the decline. War raged as Albanians, Serbs, Macedonians, Croats, Bulgarians, Turks and many others fought to create their own nations.

In the midst of death and despair, in the town of Skopje, now the capital of North

Macedonia, there was a glimmer of happiness. A child was born on 26th August, who would go on to become a symbol of love and compassion for the entire world one day.

This child was lovingly named Agnes by her parents, Nikola and Drana Bojaxhiu, who were of Albanian descent. Agnes grew up in a home filled with love and laughter. She played with her elder brother Lazar and sister Aga, attended school and went to church. She was lovingly called Gonxha, or Rosebud, by all.

Agnes's parents often helped their neighbours who were in need. One day her mother called Agnes. "Hurry, Gonxha, we have to go see Aunt Alketa. She's sick again,"

While her mother gave the ailing woman medicine, Agnes looked after her baby.

On the way back home, Agnes was deep in thought. "Nana, why does Alketa keep falling ill?"

"They are very poor. She often doesn't eat so that there is enough for the children," her mother replied.

Agnes could not imagine what it was like to go without food. "There must be so many who suffer like this. I wish I could do something for them."

The values of care and service were taking shape in her young mind.

Nikola was keen that his daughters receive as good an education as his son. One evening, when they were all gathered in the living room, he told Agnes, "You should study well. You won't realise how important it is until you are much older."

"I will, Baba. I want to be a teacher when I grow up," replied Agnes, her eyes shining.

"Good! You can help those who aren't as lucky as you," said her proud father.

Nikola's work and travel were often connected to politics. Once he had to attend a meeting in Belgrade to discuss Albanian independence. The night before he left, the family gathered around the table to pray together, as always. This was Agnes's favourite time of the day.

The next morning Nikola left with the hope of returning in a week. A few days later, a

strange carriage made its way to the house. The family ran to the gates, curious about who the unexpected visitors could be. They were shocked to see Nikola being carried out from the carriage by two men. He could hardly walk, and looked pale and weak.

The men accompanying him said they were from the Italian consulate. Apparently,

Nikola had collapsed during talks, so they had rushed him home. Lazar went to fetch a doctor. Drana realised her husband was dying and sent Agnes to call the priest.

Agnes hurried to the church. Unfortunately, their parish priest was away. But another priest had been spotted at the railway station a while ago. There was a slim chance that he could still be waiting for his train.

Agnes ran as fast as her eight-year-old legs could carry her. Her heart was pounding in her chest and her cheeks were flushed as she made her way to the station. People were hurrying up and down the platform. Agnes weaved her way through the crowd, her eyes searching desperately. Finally, she found a man dressed in a priest's robes sitting on a bench.

"Father, please, will you come to our house? My Baba is very ill," she pleaded.

"I have a train to catch, my child," replied the startled priest.

"But our priest is away and Nana says we must have a priest," Agnes said, with tears welling up in her eyes.

The priest could not refuse Agnes. He accompanied her home and recited prayers from the Bible for Nikola. The next day Nikola died in the hospital. All the people that her parents had helped came to the funeral to comfort the family.

Life for the Bojaxhiu family changed drastically following Nikola's death. Drana was inconsolable and despondent. Agnes and Aga found solace in singing in the church choir.

A few months later a letter arrived with more bad news. Nikola's partner had taken all the money from the business, leaving them broke.

Drana put on a brave face for her children and started a business in textiles. Soon many people started buying her beautiful embroidery. "It's good work. It's not heroic, but I make sure you can live comfortably," Drana told her children one day.

Agnes peeked out of the book she was reading about St. Therese, the patron saint of missionaries. "That is what St Therese says too. Even the smallest work is good as long as you do it with love." Agnes was inspired by the life of St. Therese.

Drana and Agnes continued to help those in need. Agnes realised that though she couldn't cure the sick, she could make them feel loved and wanted.

At the age of twelve, on a family pilgrimage to the shrine of the Black Madonna in Letnice, Agnes resolved to become a missionary and help people.

The opportunity came six years later. Agnes had gone to the church library to listen to a missionary who had worked in India. She was moved by his talk.

Later she spoke to the priest. "Father Jambrekovic, please tell me, can I go as a missionary to India?"

"It will be very hard work. You will have to leave your home forever. Are you sure the thought of this work makes you happy?"

"Yes, yes! It does make me happy!" Agnes said without any hesitation.

"Apply to the Loreto Order then. They have a mission in India."

Filled with purpose, Agnes hurried home to her mother. "I've decided to go to India as a missionary, Nana. I will be sorry to leave you, but I feel I must do this."

"A missionary in India? Let me think about this, Gonxha," her mother said.

Drana spent the day in her room, praying and searching for an answer. She came out the next day, calm and composed. "You are doing the best that you can, Gonxha. Put your hand in God's hand and walk all the way."

Agnes applied to the Loreto Order and was accepted. She had to go to Ireland first to learn English, then she would be sent to India.

The day of her departure arrived. Agnes stood on the platform, on the threshold of a new life. Drana and Aga had come to see her off. The shrill whistle of the train signalled that it was time to leave.

"Goodbye! I will always remember and love you all." Agnes's heart was overwhelmed with emotions as she boarded the train.

"Always look ahead, Agnes. If you look back, you will turn back." her mother's parting words held a lot of significance. Agnes would never see her family again. She was just eighteen years old!

Agnes landed half a world away in Calcutta and then travelled to Loreto Convent in Darjeeling for her training. In 1931, Agnes took her first vows as a nun at this convent. She changed her name to Sister Teresa, after St. Therese who had first inspired her to be a missionary.

Sister Teresa taught at the convent and became a popular teacher. She learnt Hindi and Bengali to better communicate with the local people. She also volunteered at a clinic for those who could not afford doctors.

Sister Teresa took her final vows in 1937 at a ceremony in Darjeeling. She was now Mother Teresa. Mother lived in the Loreto Convent in Entally, Calcutta. She taught at St. Mary's School next door.

She also began teaching at a small Bengali-medium school named St. Teresa's. On her first day at school, Mother was appalled to see the state of the classroom. The floor was dirty, the tables and desks were layered with dust, and cobwebs hung from every corner.

"How can you learn anything in this dirt?" She picked up a broom and began to clean, much to the surprise of her students. They soon joined her and the classroom was spick and span in no time.

The children had never seen a teacher like her before. They began calling her 'Ma'. A few days later, they invited their teacher to come and have tea with them. This was the

first time Mother was actually going to a slum. She saw how the poor lived, in small, bare, overcrowded and run-down shanties. The poverty and suffering of the people left a deep impression on her.

Over the next few years, Mother became more and more absorbed in the work at St. Mary's School. By 1944 she had become the principal of the school.

Outside the walls of the convent, India's struggle for independence had reached its pinnacle. The British were finally leaving India, but the country was going to be partitioned into India and Pakistan.

On 16th August, 1946, huge riots broke out in Calcutta. Armed mobs clashed, looting and killing everyone in their paths. People were afraid to step out of their homes. Supplies were limited and soon the convent ran out of food. Mother Teresa decided to bravely venture out to find food. She was about to leave when, suddenly, a man jumped over the walls of the convent and entered inside. He seemed badly injured. "Hide me, please, or the mob outside will kill me," he pleaded.

"Don't worry, I will dress your wounds and then help you get home," assured Mother Teresa.

"I don't think you should go out, Mother, it is not safe," warned a nun who overheard her.

"I cannot let our three hundred children starve. Let me go," said Mother resolutely.

The moment the violent mob moved away from their street, they stepped out. The mob had left behind a trail of death and destruction. They walked quickly, in the opposite direction from the mob. Once it seemed safer, Mother sent the man home and went to look for supplies. But all the shops were shut.

Just then, an army truck that was patrolling the area stopped in front of her. "What are you doing?" a British soldier asked in surprise. "The mobs are attacking everyone they see. It is very dangerous for you to be out."

"I came looking for food. There isn't any left for the children of the convent," explained Mother Teresa.

The soldiers persuaded her to go back, and offered to drive her home, but she refused to return empty-handed.

"We will give you some of our food. Now will you get in the truck?" said the soldier at last.

When they reached the convent, the men unloaded the sacks of supplies.

"Here we are. I don't know if you are very brave or just very stubborn, Mother," replied the soldier.

Mother simply smiled and said, "Bless you!"

A few months later Mother Teresa was on her way to Darjeeling by train. A cool breeze blew as pine forests and snow-clad mountains rushed past her window. Out of the blue, she heard a voice. "Leave the convent. Give up its comfort and safety. Follow me to the slums, among the poorest of the poor."

Startled, Mother looked around, but it was clear that the voice was speaking only to her.

In Darjeeling she made up her mind to follow the divine call. Back in Calcutta, she went to Father Celeste van Exem for advice. He was convinced of her sincerity and asked her to write to the Archbishop of Calcutta for guidance. In reply, she was asked to wait for some time. While she waited, Mother Teresa was haunted by her call. Once, a powerful vision swept across her mind – Mary, the mother of Jesus Christ, spoke to her, urging her to take care of the poor. Two years later, in 1948, her request to leave the convent was granted by the Pope himself.

Mother left for Patna to train in nursing and first aid. She started wearing coarse white sarees with blue borders, similar to the ones worn by municipal cleaners in Calcutta. Once she completed her training, she went to live with the Little Sisters of the Poor in Calcutta. Now she could finally follow her call. She decided to go to a slum called Motijheel, the poorest locality, and teach the children there. She started an open-air school, writing alphabets in the mud and teaching hygiene through games. Her students made toys out of cardboard and learnt to knit with twigs. Soon their numbers grew.

Some of Mother's old students joined her. Mother wanted to start a dispensary and went

door to door raising money for her cause. She took on rent two small rooms, one for a free clinic for the poor and the other for the school. Her ability to translate ideas into actions made her unstoppable. In a year Mother Teresa had started a new order – the Missionaries of Charity. Their main building was named the 'Mother House'.

Mother Teresa strongly believed that the biggest disease is feeling unwanted. Her hospice called 'Niramal Hriday' or pure heart was for those who could not be cured. She wanted them to feel loved and comforted in their last days.

She started a colony called Shanti Nagar for those suffering from leprosy, shunned by society. Here they could live a life of dignity and earn a living by farming, spinning or carpentry.

Mother felt the suffering around her deep within herself. But she never let this darkness affect her work. From 1960, Mother started opening homes all over the country.

During the opening of a Shishu Bhavan in Delhi, they had a surprise visitor – Prime Minister Pandit Jawaharlal Nehru! He had heard about the work done by the Missionaries of Charity and had come to visit.

Her fame had spread not only in India, but throughout the world. Many accolades were showered on her, which she accepted with great humility.

The biggest recognition of her decades of humanitarian work came in the form of the Nobel Peace Prize in 1979. The next year she received the Bharat Ratna, India's highest civilian award.

In 1982, Mother Teresa was once again in a war zone, this time in Beirut. The earth shuddered with the constant sound of bombs exploding in the background. Mother Teresa was now older and frail but she was as determined as ever. She was there on a mission – to rescue children stuck in a small hospital in the middle of the war. The thirty-seven children were mentally challenged and were perishing without food or water.

"Can't you hear the bombs? You can't just wander in there," said an army officer, shocked to see her.

"There is a lull in the firing. I must get the children out," Mother was firm.

Accompanied by the Red Cross, Mother Teresa bravely travelled through the battle-ravaged streets and an hour later returned with an ambulance filled with the children. Mother Teresa had managed the impossible!

In her lifetime, Mother established 610 missions in 123 countries. She is now officially called 'Saint Teresa of Calcutta'. She is not only the pride of India, but also one of the most enduring symbols of love in the world.

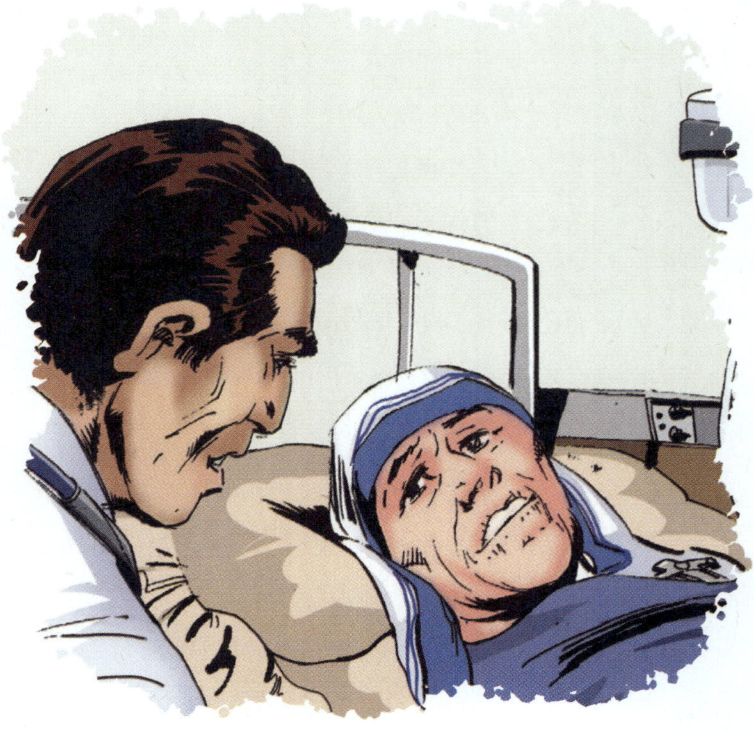

Mahatma Gandhi

Mohandas Karamchand Gandhi, the father of the nation, stirred the hearts of millions and inspired them to believe in freedom. Through the powerful weapons of Ahimsa and Satyagraha, non-violence and truth force, he brought the mighty British empire to its knees.

Mohandas was born on 2nd October, 1869, in Porbandar, a coastal town in Gujarat.

His grandfather had been a loyal and courageous dewan (minister) of the state. His father Karamchand was the dewan of Porbandar, well-known for his honesty.

His mother Putlibai was loving and deeply religious. Right from when he was little, Mohan had seen his mother observing fasts.

"Ba, why do you fast so often?" he would ask.

"For your welfare, my Moniya! I believe my prayers and fasting will bestow God's blessings on my family," she would reply.

This teaching stayed with him, and many years later, fasting became an important tool of Satyagraha.

As young boys, Mohandas and his brother Karsandas loved to play outdoors. They would roam about in the neighbourhood and climb trees for fun. One day, Mohan climbed a mango tree and was about to pluck a juicy mango. Just then, his brother pulled him down and playfully hit him. His cheeks burning red, Mohan ran home to complain to his mother.

Putlibai was sitting in front of the stove, busy making rotis for dinner. "Why didn't you just hit him back?" she asked. After all, it was natural for brothers and sisters to resolve their quarrels in this way.

Mohan was shocked. He knelt down to face his mother, and said in a pained voice, "Ba, why should I hit my brother? Shouldn't you stop him from hitting me instead of asking me to imitate him?"

Putlibai was astonished to see her Moniya thinking about right and wrong at such a tender age. She gave him a tight hug.

Mohandas's kind and gentle nature made him his mother's pet. But she was strict in the matter of studies and food. Nor did she agree with all his ideas. Once she saw him sharing some sweets with a boy named Uka. He was considered an 'untouchable' by society.

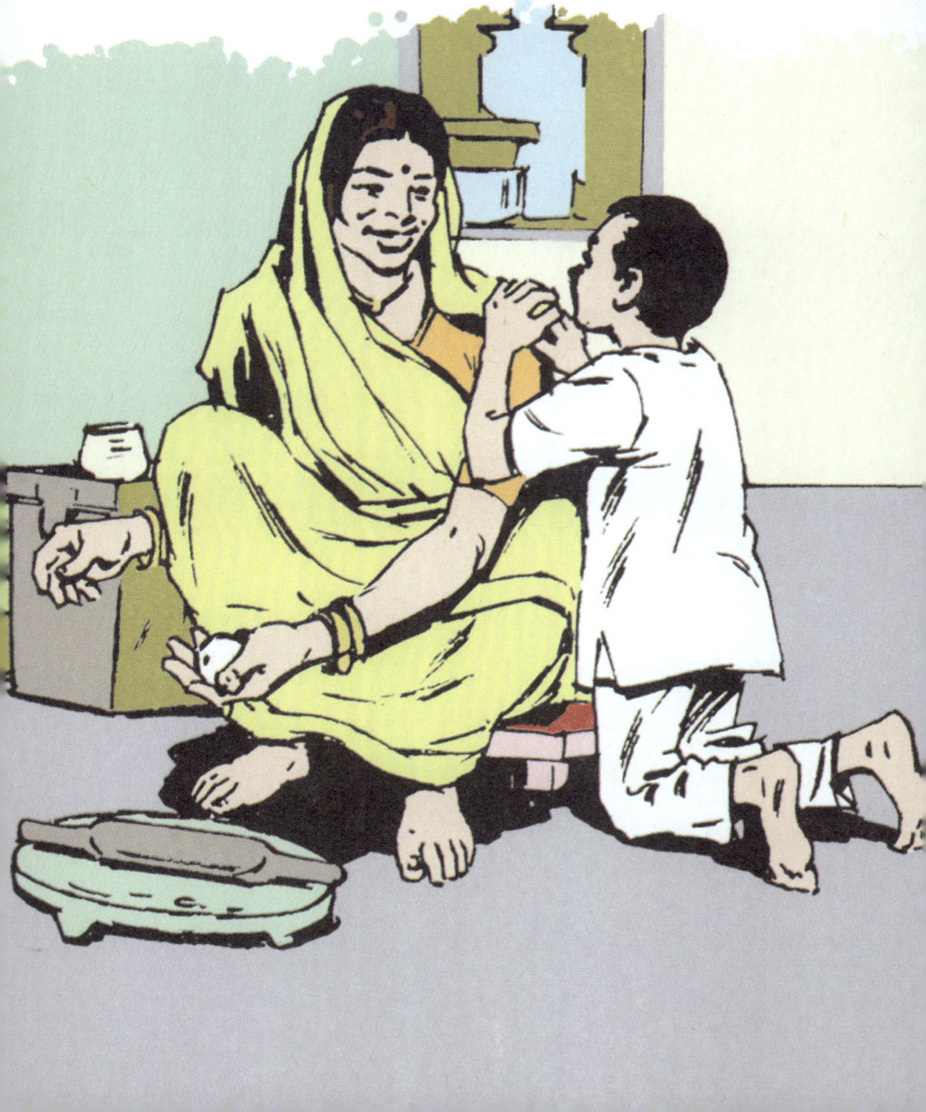

Putlibai called Mohan and scolded him. "Moniya, I just saw you touching Uka. How could you? He cleans our latrines."

"But, Ba, what's the difference between Uka and me?" asked Mohan in earnest. "If God is in all of us, then he is in Uka too."

Once again, his mother was greatly surprised by his thinking.

A few years later, Mohandas noticed his father complaining about the stockings and boots he was required to wear while attending the state durbars. "Oh God, how I hate to wear these!"

"The British want to break our pride by senselessly making us wear their kind of clothes," thought Mohan. "We must free India of them!" A mere wish at that time, it manifested into the Swadeshi movement later in his life.

Mohandas adored his parents and his love for them was further strengthened by the stories he heard in the ancient epics. How devotedly Shravana cared for his parents. How firmly Harishchandra clung to the truth. And how Rama, Sita and Lakshmana went willingly to the forest to fulfil their father's promise.

Mohandas joined the Alfred High School in Rajkot where Karamchand had taken up the post of dewan. He was a very shy and timid student.

One day, their teacher informed them that the education inspector, Mr. Giles, was coming to visit. "Be sure to make a good impression," he warned.

The British inspector arrived and looked around severely at the students. He had decided that a spelling exercise would be a good way to evaluate the class.

The students, including Mohan, bent down to their notebooks, writing the words one by one. Their anxious teacher moved about the room to see how the students were faring.

"Kettle," called out Mr. Giles.

Mohan hesitated. He scribbled the word on paper, but was not sure of the spelling. Just then he felt something prick his feet. He looked down to see a pointed boot, poking at his heel – his teacher was hovering over him. When Mohan looked up, the teacher glared at his notebook and nudged his heel again.

Actually, the teacher had noticed that Mohan had spelt 'kettle' wrong. He was trying to draw his attention to the mistake. But Mohan did not understand the hint. As a result, he was the only student who got the word wrong. The teacher later pointed out his stupidity. But it did not have any effect on an honest Mohandas.

As was the custom in those days, Mohandas was married to Kasturba when he was only thirteen. They were about the same age.

Kasturba was a lively girl and refused to let Mohan boss over her.

"I forbid you to go out today," said Mohan, who didn't want to be seen as a timid husband.

"Well, I will go! You don't listen to me when I tell you not to go out. Then why should I obey you?" With this retort, Kasturba ran out to play with her friends.

They would quarrel this way often. Though married; they were still children!

Around this time, Mohandas's elder brother got into debt. To repay the money, the two of them came up with a devious plan. They clipped a bit of gold from his brother's armlet and sold it. That evening Putlibai noticed the armlet, and began asking questions.

"It must have fallen off somewhere," lied the brothers to cover their misdeeds.

That night Mohan lay awake, tossing and turning in bed. The theft and the lie weighed on him. "I cannot carry this guilt all my life!" he thought.

The next morning, he decided to confess to his father. He felt ashamed to speak about what he had done, so he wrote down his confession on a piece of paper and handed it to his father who had taken ill.

Karamchand read the paper and tore it up. He sank back on his bed without saying a word. Tears filled his eyes. Sadness and disappointment were etched on his face.

Tears streamed down Mohandas's face. "Bapu's silent tears wound me more than a slap might have," he reflected. He saw that love could punish more effectively than violence. It was an object lesson in Ahimsa.

Often, people of various faiths would gather at his house to discuss their different points of view with Karamchand. Mohandas would listen to the conversations with interest. He developed equal respect for all religions. He came to the realisation that the one principle

common to all religions was truth. His faith in truth grew stronger from year to year. Many years later he went on to say, "Truth is God. It is a God that anyone can worship."

Karamchand, who had been ailing for a long time, died in 1885. The elders in the family, made plans for the future of his sons. It was decided that Mohandas should go to England and prepare for a career in law. With great difficulty, the family raised the money. Kasturba gave up her wedding jewellery to fund her husband's studies.

Putlibai was worried about her son travelling to a foreign land. To put her mind at rest, Mohan vowed to stay away from wine, women and meat.

At eighteen years of age, Mohandas set sail to London from Bombay. First time in a foreign land, he found everything strange and different from back home. Wanting to adapt to the English society, he began to dress in well-tailored suits like the Englishmen. He took dancing, violin and elocution lessons. He had forgotten his childhood dislike for the English in India.

Then, one day, he had a realisation – he was not going to live in England for the rest of his life. He had come here to study, and that was

his duty. From that day he transformed himself into a serious student. As his study of law progressed, he joined the inner temple of the Inns of Court in London.

All through his stay, he remained true to his vow. He became a member of the London Vegetarian Society and relished bland vegetarian food. His lifelong interest in the relationship of food with the health of body, mind and soul began here.

Mohandas returned to India in 1891.
He landed in Bombay, and was eager to meet his mother.

His brother gently broke the news to him, "Ba is no more. But she died knowing that you have passed."

"Ba... my beloved Ba!" exclaimed Mohan. He was grief-stricken, but he controlled himself. Life had to go on.

A full-fledged barrister now, Mohandas Gandhi set up his practice. But his shyness interfered. He had studied the law, but he did not know how to argue cases.

For two years he struggled to get work. Then in 1893, there came an offer that would change the course of his life.

"The trading company, Dada Abdulla & Co, wants to engage my services as a lawyer in South Africa," he announced excitedly to his family.

Gandhi soon arrived in the country of coalmines, sugar plantations, bountiful fruit and grain. His employer, Dada Abdulla Sheth, was there to receive him.

The keenly observant Mohandas realised at once that Indians were not given much respect there. But he was yet to experience first-hand the inhumanity of South Africa.

In the second week of his arrival, Gandhi was travelling for work from Durban to Pretoria. He was seated in the first-class compartment of the train.

Shortly after, the train conductor arrived and looked at him with contempt. "Hey, coolie, you can't sit here. Go to the van compartment."

Mohandas was taken aback, but he replied calmly, "I hold a first-class ticket. This is my rightful seat."

"You won't, eh? We'll see about that!"

A constable was called, who dragged a protesting Mohandas to the door and threw him out of the train with bag and baggage.

The train steamed away, leaving him on the platform. He was forced to spend the night in the dark and lonely waiting room. He shivered with cold and trembled with humiliation.

Gandhi took this experience to heart and resolved that he would fight the injustices against Indians. With this aim in mind, he gathered a group of Indian merchants in Pretoria. They would meet often to discuss their problems.

Mohandas concentrated first on finishing the legal work he had come to do. He settled

Dada Abdulla's case successfully and prepared to return to India.

His Indian friends had arranged a farewell party for him. During the party, Gandhi read in the papers that the government was taking away the voting rights of Indians. "Taking away our voting rights strikes at the root of our self-respect. You must fight it," he advised.

The others agreed with him, but they did not know how to proceed.

"Gandhi bhai, we are uneducated men. What do we understand of these matters?" said Abdulla. "If you can stay back and guide us, we will fight."

Everyone at the gathering began to plead with him to stay.

"All right, I will delay my departure," said Mohandas, giving in.

The farewell party transformed into a public committee. A polite but firm petition was drawn up and sent to the legislative assembly.

On the day of the reading of the bill, the legislative assembly hall was overflowing with Indians, newly awakened to their rights.

The shy boy was slowly transforming into a leader. The Indians, with him at the helm, formed the Natal Indian Congress in 1894.

Realising he was here for a long struggle, Gandhi brought his wife and children to

South Africa. While in India, he had spoken about the cause of South African Indians. This angered some of the locals in South Africa. They spotted Gandhi at the port and began to pelt stones at him. He was helpless against the mob. At that moment, the police superintendent's wife, Mrs. Alexander, was passing by. She bravely opened her parasol and shielded him from the blows.

The police arrived and escorted him to the police station.

Mr. Escombe, Natal's Attorney General, came to see Gandhi. "You are badly wounded. Name your assailants and I will have them arrested and prosecuted."

"No, I don't want to prosecute anyone," replied Gandhi. "They are not to blame. Their leaders and a racist society are to blame." He stuck to the principles of Ahimsa.

Gandhi settled in Transvaal's premier city, Johannesburg. Later, his English friend Henry

Polak and Indian visitors often lived together as members of Gandhi's extended family.

One day, Polak gave Gandhi a book, Unto This Last, by the great writer John Ruskin. He advocated a life of labour and simplicity, close to nature, as the life worth living. Gandhi decided to put Ruskin's ideals into practice. He chose a site for his first ashram on the outskirts of Durban, named Phoenix.

"This is our new home, and this community will be our family," he told Kasturba.

A small group of family and friends joined the ashram. They built simple houses for themselves and cultivated the land. Gandhi started a weekly newspaper, Indian Opinion, to carry on his fight against racial laws.

The Transvaal government introduced a humiliating law requiring all Indians to register themselves and obtain a personal certificate bearing their thumb impression, like criminals.

Gandhi called for a meeting of Indians in Johannesburg. "Let us pledge ourselves in

the name of God to never submit to this law," he said in his rousing speech. "Even if all others go back on the pledge and I am left alone, I will die, but never submit to the inhumane law."

Every man in the hall was charged up and ready to follow this call, like troops following a general in a non-violent war.

The struggle was called 'Passive Resistance' but Gandhi did not like the phrase. He advertised a prize in his weekly paper for another suitable name. His nephew Maganlal wrote in with a suggestion: 'Sadagraha' (firmness in a good cause).

Gandhi thought it was an excellent name. He made a small modification. "We are fighting injustice and oppression with the spiritual weapon of truth. We will therefore call it Satyagraha," he wrote. "Firmness in fighting injustice by truthful means."

When the new law was passed, Satyagraha against it commenced. A majority of Indians refused to apply for the certificates. Hundreds of them, including Gandhi, were sent to jail. But it did not weaken their resolve. They called the prison 'His Majesty's Hotel'.

Gandhi met General Smuts, the home minister, who promised to repeal the law if Indians voluntarily registered. But Smut went back on his word.

Gandhi planned a unique protest. He asked every Indian to assemble on a public ground. A large cauldron was lit. He gave an inspiring speech and threw his voluntary certificate in the burning flames.

"By burning the certificates, we declare our resolution to not submit to the act!," he said.

Following his actions, everyone in the gathering burnt their certificates.

Gandhi and many of his compatriots were imprisoned and were given harsh treatment. They had to break stones, dig fields and clean toilets. The Satyagrahis bore it without ill will. The prisoner's cap worn by Gandhi during this time has found a place in history. It is considered to be the origin of the famous khadi 'Gandhi cap'.

When Gandhi was released from jail, he started another ashram in Transvaal called Tolstoy Farm. Gandhi's family, and the families of the Satyagrahis in jail, lived a very simple life of few needs and labour for all. Later in life, Gandhi remembered the two and a half years there as the happiest period in his life. Out of this experience grew Gandhi's famous Satyagraha Ashram in Ahmedabad which was later called Sabarmati Ashram.

Meanwhile, the government's attitude towards Indians had not changed. The struggle continued. In September 1913, the third and last Satyagraha in South Africa began. This time many Indian women, including Kasturba, joined the movement. They took out processions, singing devotional songs. Kasturba was sent to jail. Gandhi led a march of about two thousand Indians from Natal to Transvaal, protesting against the unjust tax that indentured labourers settled in Natal had to pay. At last, the government yielded to the moral power of Satyagraha. Smuts accepted all the demands of Gandhi.

Gandhi had been in South Africa for twenty-one years and contributed to the welfare of his fellow Indians. Now it was time to go home. On January 1915, Mohandas Gandhi, dressed in all white – dhoti, frock-coat and traditional turban – disembarked at Bombay's Apollo Bunder port.

***

Gandhi was seated on the floor, in the veranda of his cottage. He was clad in a white khadi dhoti and wore circular-rimmed spectacles. As his one hand turned the spinning wheel, a thin delicate yarn emerged, which he pulled gently with his other hand. He looked up to see the river Sabarmati flowing peacefully, a little distance away. The birds chirped and squirrels scampered from tree to tree. As the wheel hummed gently, Gandhi's mind wandered back to the time he had started the Satyagraha Ashram.

Gandhi had just returned to Bombay from South Africa. He had gone to meet his political guide Gopal Krishna Gokhale. He advised Gandhi to travel across India for a year to get to know the people better.

While touring, Gandhi had set up an ashram in Kochrab on the outskirts of Ahmedabad. Later they had shifted to this spot on the western banks of the river Sabarmati, closer to the Sabarmati jail.

Simple white cottages with thatched roofs, sparsely furnished rooms, and uncluttered, green public spaces – the ashram was in keeping with his philosophy of simple living and high thinking.

The senior members dedicated themselves to the service of the country and took eight vows to make themselves fit for it: "I shall stand

firmly by truth, ahimsa, brahmacharya, control of the palate, non-stealing, non-possession, swadeshi and fearlessness, and stand against untouchability."

Gandhi smiled when he remembered the time he had invited a family of 'untouchables' to live at the ashram. He lovingly called them 'harijan' or people of God. It had created a flutter among the members, but they had finally let go of their prejudices and welcomed the family.

Life in the ashram followed a strict discipline. Fixed hours of morning and evening prayers. Several hours of manual labour, besides spinning, weaving, scavenging and cleaning latrines. This was his way of teaching his non-violent army to feel one with the lowest class in society. Life in the ashram was like an oasis of peace in those turbulent times.

After he had toured the country, Gandhi had plunged into politics with a passionate speech at the Banaras Hindu University. He had spoken about what he had seen in his travels – the extremes of luxury and poverty, ignorance of the people, and indifference to cleanliness. He also spoke about the revolutionary movement spreading among the educated youth.

India heard about his speech and knew that a different kind of leader had entered the political scene. Rabindranath Tagore called him 'Mahatma', the great soul. But it was in

Champaran that he was first called 'Bapu', a leader who was like a father to his people.

One Day, a farmer from the Champaran district of Bihar had come to meet Gandhi with a plea for help. "Mahatmaji, our English landlords forced us to grow Indigo. Now that synthetic Indigo has been discovered, they force us to pay them compensation for not growing it any longer." He urged Gandhi to accompany him to his village.

Gandhi finally agreed. "I want to see the condition of the farmers with my own eyes."

Mahatma Gandhi's arrival was not liked by the British government and he was ordered to leave Champaran. But he refused, and was summoned to court. The news spread like wildfire around the village. A large crowd gathered outside the court in support. Men were chanting slogans, calling him 'Bapu... Bapu... Bapu.'

Gandhi succeeded in confounding the magistrate and was quickly released. He painstakingly worked to make the landlords return part of what they had forcibly taken from the peasants. He also set up primary schools and began a programme of cleanliness in Champaran's villages.

Gandhi took up the cause of Ahmedabad's poorly paid mill workers next. They pledged to continue the strike till the mill owners agreed to a raise. The mill owners were adamant, and the workers began to tire. Gandhi sensed a lack of unity among them and was afraid

they would give up. He thought of an idea to convince them.

The next day he called a meeting of the workers. "Friends, I shall not touch food because you are not united in your pledge," he stated.

The workers were shocked. "Bapu, no! Do not do this!"

"My mother would fast for our good, I want to do this for the welfare of all the workers," replied Gandhi firmly.

For the first time, through a fast, through self-denial, a leader was playing the deeply personal role of a parent. Gandhi's fast influenced the mill owners so much that they came to an agreement with the workers.

Almost immediately after this came the issue of the cultivators from the Kheda district of Gujarat. Farmers on the verge of starvation were being forced by the government to pay land revenue. Gandhi persuaded the peasants to not pay any tax. The British

confiscated the cattle, household goods and even standing crops of those who refused to pay. Finally, the courage and self-sacrifice of the people was rewarded. The government suspended the tax for the poor peasants. This was the beginning of education for the people of Gujarat in Satyagraha.

During the First World War, Gandhi helped England recruit Indian soldiers. In fair exchange for her war efforts, India wanted home rule. But at the end of the war, the British government introduced the Rowlatt Act – the harsh war-time measures of preventive indefinite detention and imprisonment without trial were to continue.

It led Gandhi to take his first major political step at an all-India level. He called for a nationwide Satyagraha. All shops, businesses, mills and factories were to be voluntarily closed on 6th April, 1919. The entire nation came to a grinding halt.

A few days later Gandhi was arrested, and as a reaction there was violence in some places. Gandhi was deeply pained. "What a great blot on Satyagraha! I have made a Himalayan miscalculation. I believed wrongly that the people would keep peace." He called it off.

The terrible massacre at Jallianwala Bagh on 13th April, 1919, sent shockwaves throughout the country. Losing his faith in the British

sense of justice, Gandhi turned into a determined rebel against British rule in India. He urged every Indian to unite against them. "Proclaim to the government: you may hang us on the gallows, you may send us to prison, but you will get no cooperation from us."

The Non-cooperation movement was based on Gandhi's belief in non-violence. It meant refusal to cooperate with the British government in any manner and involved the boycott of British courts, schools and colleges, the surrendering of British titles and the boycott of British goods.

So powerful was Gandhi's call, and so profound was the trust in him, that thousands of students left their schools and colleges and joined the national vidyapeethas. Lawyers in their hundreds gave up their practice and joined Gandhi. Among them were Motilal Nehru, Chittaranjan Das, C. Rajagopalachari, Rajendra Prasad, Vallabhbhai Patel and

Jawaharlal Nehru. They became the chief generals of Gandhi's non-violent fight for freedom.

The poverty in Indian villages disturbed Gandhi greatly. As a solution, he suggested the boycott of foreign clothes and the revival of age-old cottage industries like spinning and weaving. Khadi freed people from the cultural slavery of the English and made them conscious of themselves as Indians. This had been his dream as a boy.

Khadi became the uniform of Gandhi's non-violent army of Swaraj. Gandhi travelled for a whole year to propagate his ideas. The masses were stirred by his message. They gathered in maidans, made heaps of their foreign clothes and set them on fire.

Kasturba too was part of the movement; she took up spinning and weaving khadi and encouraged other women to do the same.

In December 1929, the Indian National Congress, with Jawaharlal Nehru presiding,

declared complete independence, or 'Purna Swaraj' as the goal of India. It resolved to launch a programme of civil disobedience, including non-payment of taxes.

The All-India Congress Committee was authorised to plan and carry out the programme, but the real decision lay with Gandhi. As a first step in the coming struggle, Gandhi asked people to take a pledge of independence: "We believe that it is the right of the Indian people to have freedom and to enjoy the fruits of their toil. The British Government has ruined India economically,

politically, culturally and spiritually. We hold it to be a crime against man and God to submit any longer to a rule that has caused this four-fold disaster to our country. We believe therefore, that India must sever the British connection and attain Purna Swaraj or complete independence."

Many came forward and took the pledge.

Gandhi took more than two months to decide how to start the battle. The government had imposed a tax on making salt, which put a heavy burden on the common man. He wrote to the Viceroy, Lord Irwin, about the suffering of Indians, and about the unjust salt tax. When his appeal did not have any effect, Gandhi decided to break the salt laws. The very simplicity of his choice made the issue more dramatic.

On 12th March, 1930, at 6.30 a.m. Gandhi addressed his band of seventy-eight Satyagrahis. "We hope to become the representatives of the poor, the lowest of the low and the weakest of the weak."

Gandhi stepped out of the Ashram clad in his white dhoti, shawl and a wooden staff in hand. His eyes were shining with determination. A shiver of excitement ran through the crowd. Gandhi walked fast, leading the long march from Sabarmati Ashram to the coastal town of Dandi in south Gujarat.

Every village and town they passed was decked with steamers or flower garlands to welcome the marchers. Men, women and children lined the roads, shouting slogans for the victory of the march.

Stopping at each place, Bapu gave the same advice to his fellow countrymen: "Spin every day and wear khadi. Abolish untouchability. Banish the evil of drink."

For twenty-four days Gandhi and his Satyagrahis marched towards the sea. Thousands of people joined the procession. Newspapers and the radio carried news about the Dandi march to every corner of India and the world.

The marchers arrived at Dandi on 5th April, covering a distance of 385 kilometres. Early next day, Gandhi and his followers stood on the beach. The Arabian Sea looked beautiful in the morning light. The foamy waves ebbed and flowed, leaving salt crystals on the shore. Gandhi bent down, picked up a handful of salt

... IF INDIA IS TO LIVE AS A NATION,
THE SLOW DEATH BY STARVATION
OF HER PEOPLE IS TO STOP, SOME
REMEDY MUST BE FOUND. IF MY
LETTER MAKES NO APPEAL TO
YOUR HEART, I SHALL PROCEED
WITH SUCH CO-WORKERS OF
THE ASHRAM I CAN TAKE, TO
DISREGARD THE PROVISIONS OF
THE SALT LAWS.

and held it up. "With this, I am shaking the foundation of the British Empire!" he declared with joy.

Shouts of "Mahatma Gandhi ki jay" and "Vande Mataram" filled the air.

This simple act of defiance proved to be immensely powerful. Salt became the symbol of India's nationalistic spirit and will to freedom – for it sought to reclaim what belonged to the nation. The making of illegal salt became a way of protest along the coast.

The British government, alarmed by this mass defiance, responded with force. But no matter how many salt pans they destroyed, or how many people they beat up and arrested, the movement did not stop. Gandhi encouraged more women to join the Satyagraha. They gathered outside liquor shops and shops selling foreign cloth, and appealed to the public to boycott these things.

One year later, the Gandhi-Irwin pact was signed. Out of the many demands the British accepted, one was that Indians could make their own salt. This was a huge victory for Ahimsa and Satyagraha.

Over the next few years Gandhi carried forward the freedom struggle. Throughout his lifetime, He was arrested and jailed many times. But every time he emerged with a stronger determination to fight the British.

Gandhi strove for the removal of untouchability from all walks of life. He built a small cottage for himself at Sevagram, Maharashtra, where he dedicated himself to the revival of the dying village craft industries.

In September 1939, the Second World War broke out. The Congress asked for the promise of freedom after the war in return for help in the war effort. The British offered a Constitution formed by Indians, but it also gave provinces and princes the option to keep out of the new government. This would lead to a fragmented India. The Congress leaders rejected the offer.

On 8th August, 1942, The All-India Congress Committee met in Bombay and launched the Quit India movement. They demanded the immediate end of British rule in India.

Gandhi addressed the rally with the powerful message. "Do or Die! We shall either free India or die in the attempt." Thus began a mass struggle of non-violence on the largest scale under the leadership of Gandhi.

On 15th August, 1947, India declared independence at the stroke of midnight. The efforts of Mahatma Gandhi, of freedom fighters and of every Indian who had joined the freedom movement had finally borne fruit.

Independence also came with the partition of India, which deeply saddened Gandhi. Partition led to widespread communal riots, lootings and killings. At seventy-eight years, in spite of ill health, Gandhi went on an indefinite fast in Calcutta and later in Delhi, till the community leaders promised to give up violence.

But Gandhi's efforts to unite the people were not liked by everyone. At 5.10 p.m.

on 30th January, 1948, on his way to the evening prayer meeting, Gandhi was shot dead. The light that had illuminated millions of hearts had gone out. But as Prime Minister Jawaharlal Nehru said in his tribute: 'He lives in the hearts of millions and he will live for immortal ages.'